01/01/16

Dear Pat —
Thank you for
all your support
For your ...
Wendy

D0030322

The Gratitude Habit

...A 365 Day Journal and Workbook

*A tool for increasing positive
feelings in your daily life*

Wendy Meg Siegel

Copyright © 2012 by Wendy Meg Siegel
WendyArts.com

All Rights Reserved.
No part of this book may be reproduced in any form without
permission in writing from the author, with the exception of
brief excerpts for review purposes or personal use by the
purchaser of this book.

Printed in the United States of America

First Printing, 2012

ISBN-13: 978-1480226401
ISBN-10: 1480226408

Cover Photo by Wendy Meg Siegel
WendyArts.com

With love and appreciation to
Eric and Melissa
for their support and feedback, and for
adding so much joy and richness to my life.

Much thanks to my parents
for a lifetime of love and
encouragement, and for
always believing in me.

About Gratitude

Thanksgiving is more than a holiday that comes once a year. It is a powerful tool that can be used in any moment, each and every day. There is always something to be thankful for, no matter how challenging life may become at times. Cultivating your relationship with gratitude is a simple path to improving the quality of your life and experiencing more joy and happiness, everyday.

Gratitude is a feeling of appreciation for all that you have in your life, all that you will have, and all that you are. It is the expression of thanksgiving for the things that make life worth living and for the hidden blessings that are often overlooked. It is being able to say "thank you" for the little things that make you smile and for those that add joy to living. It is an appreciation for your life circumstances being as good as they are and not any worse. It is being able to express thanks for the people you see each day and for those you carry in your heart. And as you will see as you use this journal, its effects are profound.

In childhood, we are taught to say "thank you" when someone says something kind or helps us out. We are encouraged to write thank you notes for the gifts we receive. So we grow up with a superficial experience of gratitude, rather than a deeper understanding of the powerful and positive force gratitude can be in our lives.

As grownups, we find ourselves in a fast-paced world where the common focus is often on what we lack and what we think is wrong or missing in our lives. By concentrating on the negatives, we not only amplify our perception of what is wrong but we end up overlooking many of our gifts. With a simple shift in perspective, and by seeing the world through the eyes of gratitude, we can instead amplify our awareness of all the good in our lives.

You can easily develop a gratitude habit. It takes very little to begin incorporating gratitude into your life — just some determination and a couple of minutes a day to write down 2 to 5 items you appreciate. Soon after you start, you will be surprised at how your mind automatically finds things to include in your journal. Rather than focusing on life's struggles and unmet expectations, you will view situations and events more optimistically. In fact, it may seem as if you have put on a new pair of glasses that allows you to see with greater clarity and awareness.

> *If you try to count your blessings you are likely to find that they are too numerous to count, and your troubles are relatively few in comparison.*

Our lives are filled with large and small gifts but most of them do not come to us wrapped with a bow. The loving hug from a favorite aunt, the neighbor who says just the right thing at exactly the right time, a good cup of coffee, the sound of laughter, the smell of freshly baked bread, or catching sight of a rainbow are all examples of the many simple gifts of life. The ability to give thanks and truly appreciate our many blessings not only carries with it the advantage of a greater sense of happiness but also attracts more blessings to be thankful for.

We are habitual by nature, and for good reason. Habits allow us to manage the huge number of choices we need to make on a daily basis. Habits can be very powerful allies when we intentionally create them. Research shows that we form habits over time, through repetition, whether positive or negative. Once gratitude becomes a habit, our unconscious mind naturally creates positive feelings and happier thoughts.

Relationship to Gratitude

Before beginning this journal, take a few minutes to reflect on your personal relationship with gratitude. Use the following questions as prompts for writing anything that comes to mind.

What is gratitude to you? What does it mean to live in gratitude? What is your past history with gratitude? How would you like to develop your relationship with gratitude? What do you hope to get out of this book?

_____

_____

_____

_____

_____

_____

_____

_____

Gratitude Journals

A gratitude journal can be used in just minutes a day and provide many benefits in the process. It can train your mind to keep things in perspective; to shift focus from the everyday troubles and problems of daily life, to the blessings that fill each day. It can become a wonderful reminder of all the little and special things you have to be grateful for. Even more so, working with this journal will help you develop a habit of naturally and spontaneously focusing on the good things in your life.

Benefits of Keeping a Gratitude Journal

How often have you spent time worrying about something that may or may not happen in the future? Have you ever lost sleep over negative thoughts and concerns? Our thoughts affect our mood, and thoughts of gratitude have the power to improve our sense of emotional well-being.

Research shows that people who make gratitude a part of their lives are happier and more joyful than those who have not. They are more optimistic and feel better about themselves and their lives. Even those with chronic health issues have been found to sleep better and look at their lives more optimistically after practicing gratitude. The more you make gratitude a part of your life, the easier it is to have some choice as to which direction your mind goes.

Focusing on gratitude:

- Helps develop a more positive overall outlook.
- Reduces stress and anxiety.
- Increases the presence of joy and happiness.
- Improves the quality of life.

- Increases awareness of your many blessings.
- Helps shift your mind's focus from problems to gifts.
- Helps develop the habit of gratitude, allowing it to become an automatic daily presence.
- Helps prioritize what's important in life.
- Supports letting go of worries and challenges.
- Improves physical and mental health.

When to use a gratitude journal: You can use your gratitude journal at any time that works best with your schedule. When are you most likely to be able to utilize your journal on a regular basis? By writing in the morning, you have the advantage of infusing your day with positive energy. Journaling your thankful thoughts at the end of the day can help you go to sleep with a smile in your heart, improving the quality of your sleep. For those who would like to give their day a boost, consider writing your gratitudes in the middle of the day. Whether you journal once a day or multiple times throughout the day, you are likely to experience greater feelings of calm and optimism.

> *Start your day with gratitude.*
> *First thing each morning, give thanks*
> *for the many blessings in your life.*

Start your day off right: Upon awakening, spend a couple of quiet minutes of gratitude whether or not you choose to write in your journal at that time. Give thanks for the day ahead, for another day to experience the adventure of life. Appreciate anything or anyone that comes to mind. Although the practice of morning gratitude does not take long, the effects can last throughout the day.

What You Will Find in this Journal

Here's what's included:

- 365 gratitude journal entries.
- Workbook exercises.
- *100 Gratitudes* list — pages for listing 100 people, places, and things you most appreciate.
- Gratitude prompts, thoughts, and reminders.
- Activities and techniques you can use to help deepen a gratitude habit.
- Writing activities and exercises.
- Blank writing pages.
- List of ideas for keeping gratitude active in your life after completing this journal.
- *Gratitude Action Plan* — space to establish a plan for how to keep gratitude present in your life.
- *Quotes and Notes* — pages to record any quotes you come across that you would like to reference.

Journal entries: There are 365 entries allowing you to start on any day of the year. If you miss one or more days, at any point, you can continue without leaving blank pages. Pick it up again whenever you wish to resume using the gratitude journal. You may decide to use this journal daily over the course of a year or record your blessings periodically. You may prefer to journal once or twice a week, or to fill the entire book within one month. Make this journal your own, and use it in the way you find most beneficial.

Workbook entries: Incorporated throughout the journal are questions, writing prompts, gratitude activities, etc. The workbook aspect of this journal is designed to help you develop a more in-depth relationship with gratitude and to increase your awareness of how much there is to appreciate. Although the workbook activities are intended to be completed in this book, you may prefer a separate notebook, folder or computer file for your additional gratitude writing.

Suggested steps for using your journal/workbook:

- Choose a time of day to use the journal that fits your schedule.
- Keep the journal in an easily accessible location.
- Notice all the gifts, large and small, that come into your life throughout each day.
- Take time to write in the daily journal entries.
- Complete the workbook entries when you come to them. Use these as prompts as you continue through the journal.
- Review your journal entries when you are feeling sad, depressed, or need a positive boost. Use it as a reminder of the good things in life.

Happiness is not based on the occasional grand things that happen in your life. It comes from acknowledging the steady flow of moments to appreciate.

So Much to Be Grateful For

Two feelings or thoughts cannot occupy the same place at the same time. When you are immersed in appreciation, it is hard to stay wrapped up in life's dramas, sadness and feelings of lack. Gratitude can transport your mind away from troubles to a positive place of acceptance and greater peace. We tend to smile when thinking of the good things in life and it's hard to hold onto negative feelings when smiling. So, remember to find things to smile about. Here's a way to begin.

Challenge yourself to write 100 things you are thankful for. Complete the list before you begin this journal, or get the list started now and add to it as you go through the journal pages. The **100 Gratitudes** list is a wonderful reference for any time you need a positive reminder of the many gifts that fill your life. You will find a second list at the back of this book to use once you have completed the journal.

Here are some ideas to help you get started with your list of **100 Gratitudes**:

Think of anything you love and enjoy... people, places, pets, nature, vacations, holidays, events, books, movies, songs, food, sports, creative experiences, physical attributes, things that make you feel happy and joyful, things that make you feel comfortable or peaceful, jobs and financial security, the seasons, a special day, things that warm your heart, things that enrich your life, the basics, the small and simple things of life, or something you often take for granted...sunshine, moonlight, the comfortable chair, running water, and smiles.

100 Gratitudes

Before beginning the journal, make a list of 100 different items you are grateful for, without repetition. What do you appreciate most in your life?

I am grateful for:

1.

2.

3.

4.

5.

6.

7.

8.

9.

10.

11.

12.

13.

14.

15.

16.

17.

18.

19.

20.

21.

22.

23.

24.

25.

26.

27.

28.

29.

30.

I am grateful for:

31.

32.

33.

34.

35.

36.

37.

38.

39.

40.

41.

42.

43.

44.

45.

46.

47.

48.

49.

50.

51.

52.

53.

54.

55.

56.

57.

58.

59.

60.

61.

62.

63.

64.

65.

I am grateful for:

66.

67.

68.

69.

70.

71.

72.

73.

74.

75.

76.

77.

78.

79.

80.

81.

82.

83.

84.

85.

86.

87.

88.

89.

90.

91.

92.

93.

94.

95.

96.

97.

98.

99.

100.

Daily Gratitude Journal

*Give thanks for each new day even
though it happens every 24 hours.*

Day 1   **Date:**

_____
_____
_____
_____
_____

Day 2   **Date:**

_____
_____
_____
_____
_____

Day 3   **Date:**

_____
_____
_____
_____
_____

Day 4   Date:

_____

_____

_____

_____

_____

Day 5   Date:

_____

_____

_____

_____

_____

Day 6   Date:

_____

_____

_____

_____

_____

Day 7   Date:

_____

_____

_____

_____

_____

Day 8   Date:

_____

_____

_____

_____

_____

Day 9   Date:

_____

_____

_____

_____

_____

Day 10   Date:

_____

_____

_____

_____

_____

Day 11   Date:

_____

_____

_____

_____

_____

Day 12   Date:

_____
_____
_____
_____
_____

Day 13   Date:

_____
_____
_____
_____
_____

Day 14   Date:

_____
_____
_____
_____
_____

What is going right in your life?
What is exactly as you would want it to be?

_____
_____
_____
_____
_____

Day 15   Date:

_____

_____

_____

_____

Day 16   Date:

_____

_____

_____

_____

Day 17   Date:

_____

_____

_____

_____

Day 18   Date:

_____

_____

_____

_____

Day 19   Date:

_____
_____
_____
_____
_____

Day 20   Date:

_____
_____
_____
_____
_____

Day 21   Date:

_____
_____
_____
_____
_____

Name five people you are thankful for today.

1. _____
2. _____
3. _____
4. _____
5. _____

Day 22   Date:

_____

_____

_____

_____

_____

Day 23   Date:

_____

_____

_____

_____

_____

Day 24   Date:

_____

_____

_____

_____

_____

Day 25   Date:

_____

_____

_____

_____

_____

Day 26   Date:

_____
_____
_____
_____
_____

Day 27   Date:

_____
_____
_____
_____
_____

Day 28   Date:

_____
_____
_____
_____
_____

Who brings happiness into your life?
Who makes you smile just by thinking of them?

_____
_____
_____
_____
_____

Day 29   Date:

_____
_____
_____
_____
_____

Day 30   Date:

_____
_____
_____
_____
_____

Day 31   Date:

_____
_____
_____
_____
_____

Day 32   Date:

_____
_____
_____
_____
_____

Day 33   Date:

_____
_____
_____
_____
_____

Day 34   Date:

_____
_____
_____
_____

Day 35   Date:

_____
_____
_____
_____

What do you appreciate most about your friendships?

_____
_____
_____
_____
_____

*Give thanks for those who have inspired
your courage, strength, and resolve.*

Day 36   **Date:**

_____

_____

_____

_____

_____

Day 37   **Date:**

_____

_____

_____

_____

_____

Day 38   **Date:**

_____

_____

_____

_____

_____

Day 39   Date:

_____

_____

_____

_____

_____

Day 40   Date:

_____

_____

_____

_____

_____

Day 41   Date:

_____

_____

_____

_____

_____

Day 42   Date:

_____

_____

_____

_____

_____

Day 43   Date:

_____

_____

_____

_____

_____

Day 44   Date:

_____

_____

_____

_____

_____

Day 45   Date:

_____

_____

_____

_____

_____

Day 46   Date:

_____

_____

_____

_____

_____

Day 47   Date:

_____
_____
_____
_____
_____

Day 48   Date:

_____
_____
_____
_____

Day 49   Date:

_____
_____
_____
_____
_____

Write cards, notes, postcards or e-mails
to 5 people to let them know how grateful
you are to have them in your life.

You can make them as short as one or two
sentences or long enough to fill a letter.

> *Remember to take the time to appreciate yourself and all you bring to the world.*

Day 50   **Date:**

_____

_____

_____

_____

_____

Day 51   **Date:**

_____

_____

_____

_____

_____

Day 52   **Date:**

_____

_____

_____

_____

_____

Day 53   Date:

_____
_____
_____
_____
_____

Day 54   Date:

_____
_____
_____
_____
_____

Day 55   Date:

_____
_____
_____
_____
_____

Day 56   Date:

_____
_____
_____
_____
_____

Day 57   Date:

_____
_____
_____
_____
_____

Day 58   Date:

_____
_____
_____
_____
_____

Day 59   Date:

_____
_____
_____
_____
_____

Day 60   Date:

_____
_____
_____
_____
_____

Day 61   Date:

_____
_____
_____
_____
_____

Day 62   Date:

_____
_____
_____
_____
_____

Day 63   Date:

_____
_____
_____
_____
_____

What do you appreciate most about yourself?

_____
_____
_____
_____
_____

Day 64   Date:

_____

_____

_____

_____

_____

Day 65   Date:

_____

_____

_____

_____

_____

Day 66   Date:

_____

_____

_____

_____

_____

Day 67   Date:

_____

_____

_____

_____

_____

Day 68   Date:

_____
_____
_____
_____
_____

Day 69   Date:

_____
_____
_____
_____

What are you good at? What skills and abilities do
you have? Which of these do you appreciate most?

_____
_____
_____
_____
_____
_____
_____
_____
_____

Day 70   Date:

_____
_____
_____
_____
_____

Day 71   Date:

_____
_____
_____
_____
_____

Day 72   Date:

_____
_____
_____
_____
_____

Day 73   Date:

_____
_____
_____
_____
_____

Day 74   Date:

_____
_____
_____
_____
_____

Day 75   Date:

_____
_____
_____
_____
_____

Day 76   Date:

_____
_____
_____
_____
_____

Ask yourself: How can I become even more of a blessing
to others? How am I already a gift in other people's lives?

_____
_____
_____
_____
_____

Day 77   Date:

_____

_____

_____

_____

_____

Day 78   Date:

_____

_____

_____

_____

_____

Day 79   Date:

_____

_____

_____

_____

_____

Day 80   Date:

_____

_____

_____

_____

_____

Day 81   Date:

_____
_____
_____
_____
_____

Day 82   Date:

_____
_____
_____
_____

Day 83   Date:

_____
_____
_____
_____

What changes have you noticed since
you began using this journal?

_____
_____
_____
_____
_____

Day 84   Date:

_____
_____
_____
_____
_____

Day 85   Date:

_____
_____
_____
_____
_____

Day 86   Date:

_____
_____
_____
_____
_____

Day 87   Date:

_____
_____
_____
_____

Day 88   Date:

_____
_____
_____
_____
_____

Day 89   Date:

_____
_____
_____
_____
_____

Day 90   Date:

_____
_____
_____
_____
_____

Send yourself a postcard or note as a reminder
of how much there is to appreciate.

Or you may choose to write a series of four notes, all
at once. Seal and address them, and have them ready
to send one out each week for the next four weeks.

(Write about anything you appreciate.)

> *Don't let the illusion of what you think
> you are missing cloud the reality of all you have.*

Day 91   **Date:**

_____
_____
_____
_____
_____

Day 92   **Date:**

_____
_____
_____
_____
_____

Day 93   **Date:**

_____
_____
_____
_____
_____

Day 94   Date:

_____

_____

_____

_____

_____

Day 95   Date:

_____

_____

_____

_____

_____

Day 96   Date:

_____

_____

_____

_____

_____

Day 97   Date:

_____

_____

_____

_____

_____

Day 98   Date:

_____

_____

_____

_____

_____

Day 99   Date:

_____

_____

_____

_____

_____

Day 100   Date:

_____

_____

_____

_____

_____

Day 101   Date:

_____

_____

_____

_____

_____

Day 102   Date:

_____
_____
_____
_____
_____

Day 103   Date:

_____
_____
_____
_____
_____

Day 104   Date:

_____
_____
_____
_____
_____

What three things have you learned through the years
which have had the greatest impact on your life?

_____
_____
_____
_____
_____

Day 105   Date:

_____

_____

_____

_____

_____

Day 106   Date:

_____

_____

_____

_____

_____

Day 107   Date:

_____

_____

_____

_____

_____

Day 108   Date:

_____

_____

_____

_____

_____

Day 109   Date:

_____
_____
_____
_____
_____

Day 110   Date:

_____
_____
_____
_____
_____

Day 111   Date:

_____
_____
_____
_____
_____

Which memories are you most thankful for?
How have they shaped your life?

_____
_____
_____
_____
_____

Day 112   Date:

_____

_____

_____

_____

_____

Day 113   Date:

_____

_____

_____

_____

_____

Day 114   Date:

_____

_____

_____

_____

_____

Day 115   Date:

_____

_____

_____

_____

Day 116   Date:

_____
_____
_____
_____
_____

Day 117   Date:

_____
_____
_____
_____
_____

Day 118   Date:

_____
_____
_____
_____
_____

Which teachers have influenced your life?
How have they shaped the person you have become?

_____
_____
_____
_____
_____

Day 119   Date:

_____

_____

_____

_____

_____

Day 120   Date:

_____

_____

_____

_____

_____

Day 121   Date:

_____

_____

_____

_____

_____

Day 122   Date:

_____

_____

_____

_____

_____

Day 123   Date:

_____
_____
_____
_____
_____

Day 124   Date:

_____
_____
_____
_____
_____

Day 125   Date:

_____
_____
_____
_____
_____

Notice the smile of a stranger. Take the
opportunity this week, to smile at a passerby
so they can experience a moment to appreciate.

Day 126   Date:

_____

_____

_____

_____

_____

Day 127   Date:

_____

_____

_____

_____

_____

Day 128   Date:

_____

_____

_____

_____

_____

Day 129   Date:

_____

_____

_____

_____

_____

Day 130   Date:

_____
_____
_____
_____
_____

Day 131   Date:

_____
_____
_____
_____
_____

Day 132   Date:

_____
_____
_____
_____
_____

Spread your appreciation around.

- Sprinkle your gratitude where ever you go this week.

- Do something unexpected for someone just because you appreciate them.

Day 133   Date:

_____

_____

_____

_____

_____

Day 134   Date:

_____

_____

_____

_____

_____

Day 135   Date:

_____

_____

_____

_____

_____

Day 136   Date:

_____

_____

_____

_____

_____

Day 137   Date:

_____
_____
_____
_____
_____

Day 138   Date:

_____
_____
_____
_____
_____

Day 139   Date:

_____
_____
_____
_____
_____

Give thanks for any and all of your basic needs that are currently being met (food, shelter, water, shoes and clothing, etc.).

_____
_____
_____
_____

> *Many people go without enough food.*
> *They exist on very little. Give thanks*
> *for every meal and every snack*
> *you eat this week.*

Day 140   **Date:**

_____

_____

_____

_____

_____

Day 141   **Date:**

_____

_____

_____

_____

_____

Day 142   **Date:**

_____

_____

_____

_____

_____

Day 143   Date:

_____

_____

_____

_____

_____

Day 144   Date:

_____

_____

_____

_____

_____

Day 145   Date:

_____

_____

_____

_____

_____

Day 146   Date:

_____

_____

_____

_____

_____

Day 147   Date:

_____

_____

_____

_____

_____

Day 148   Date:

_____

_____

_____

_____

_____

Day 149   Date:

_____

_____

_____

_____

_____

Day 150   Date:

_____

_____

_____

_____

_____

Day 151   Date:

_____
_____
_____
_____
_____

Day 152   Date:

_____
_____
_____
_____
_____

Day 153   Date:

_____
_____
_____
_____
_____

Appreciate all the steps it takes to bring food to
your table, including your role. What are some
of the steps in the process that come to mind?

_____
_____
_____
_____

Day 154   Date:

_____
_____
_____
_____

Day 155   Date:

_____
_____
_____
_____

Day 156   Date:

_____
_____
_____
_____

Day 157   Date:

_____
_____
_____
_____

Day 158   Date:

_____
_____
_____
_____
_____

Day 159   Date:

_____
_____
_____
_____

Day 160   Date:

_____
_____
_____
_____

Consider the many people performing jobs behind the
scenes, such as collecting garbage, processing mail, and
driving trucks to move food and goods across the
country. These are people who are not often seen, yet
have an impact on your daily life. Who comes to mind?

_____
_____
_____

Day 161   Date:

_____
_____
_____
_____
_____

Day 162   Date:

_____
_____
_____
_____
_____

Day 163   Date:

_____
_____
_____
_____
_____

Day 164   Date:

_____
_____
_____
_____
_____

Day 165   Date:

_____
_____
_____
_____
_____

Day 166   Date:

_____
_____
_____
_____
_____

Spend this week noticing the many gadgets and inventions
that help you throughout the day. Acknowledge how they
benefit and support you. Appreciate their very existence
and the individuals who have invented them.

There was a time when people had to pump their own
water and carry it into their homes. Now we just turn on
the faucet. Not long ago, there were no remote controls
for the TV, and no microwave ovens or cell phones.
What household gadgets help make your life easier?
Consider what life would be like without them.

_____
_____
_____
_____
_____

Day 167   Date:

_____

_____

_____

_____

_____

Day 168   Date:

_____

_____

_____

_____

_____

Day 169   Date:

_____

_____

_____

_____

_____

Day 170   Date:

_____

_____

_____

_____

_____

Day 171   Date:

_____
_____
_____
_____
_____

Day 172   Date:

_____
_____
_____
_____
_____

Day 173   Date:

_____
_____
_____
_____
_____

What everyday items do you use regularly
that have become part of the flow of life?
(For example: pens, paper, toothbrush, spoon, etc.)

_____
_____
_____
_____

Expressing gratitude for what you already have opens the door to allow more blessings to flow into your life.

Day 174   **Date:**

_____

_____

_____

_____

_____

Day 175   **Date:**

_____

_____

_____

_____

_____

Day 176   **Date:**

_____

_____

_____

_____

_____

Day 177   Date:

_____
_____
_____
_____
_____

Day 178   Date:

_____
_____
_____
_____
_____

Day 179   Date:

_____
_____
_____
_____
_____

Day 180   Date:

_____
_____
_____
_____
_____

Day 181   Date:

_____

_____

_____

_____

_____

Day 182   Date:

_____

_____

_____

_____

_____

Day 183   Date:

_____

_____

_____

_____

_____

Day 184   Date:

_____

_____

_____

_____

Day 185   Date:

_____
_____
_____
_____
_____

Day 186   Date:

_____
_____
_____
_____

What have you longed for in the past that is now
incorporated into your life? What have you manifested?
Which of your dreams have become reality?
Give thanks for the gifts you have received.

_____
_____
_____
_____
_____
_____
_____
_____

Day 187   Date:

_____

_____

_____

_____

_____

Day 188   Date:

_____

_____

_____

_____

_____

Day 189   Date:

_____

_____

_____

_____

_____

Day 190   Date:

_____

_____

_____

_____

Day 191   Date:

_____

_____

_____

_____

_____

Day 192   Date:

_____

_____

_____

_____

Make a list of your accomplishments both large and
small. Appreciate yourself for those achievements
and the experiences you have had in the process.

_____

_____

_____

_____

_____

_____

_____

_____

Day 193   Date:

_____

_____

_____

_____

_____

Day 194   Date:

_____

_____

_____

_____

_____

Day 195   Date:

_____

_____

_____

_____

_____

Day 196   Date:

_____

_____

_____

_____

Day 197   Date:

_____
_____
_____
_____
_____

Day 198   Date:

_____
_____
_____
_____
_____

What would you like to manifest in your life?
What do you want to create for your future?

_____
_____
_____
_____
_____
_____
_____
_____
_____

Day 199   Date:

_____

_____

_____

_____

_____

Day 200   Date:

_____

_____

_____

_____

_____

Day 201   Date:

_____

_____

_____

_____

_____

Day 202   Date:

_____

_____

_____

_____

Day 203   Date:

_____

_____

_____

_____

_____

Day 204   Date:

_____

_____

_____

_____

_____

Day 205   Date:

_____

_____

_____

_____

_____

Write a letter to express gratitude for something you
want to achieve in the future, as if it has already
happened. Step into the shoes of your future self
and give thanks for what you have manifested.

(You may want to use the writing pages
in the back of this book.)

Day 260   Date:

_____
_____
_____
_____
_____

Day 261   Date:

_____
_____
_____
_____
_____

Day 262   Date:

_____
_____
_____
_____
_____

Day 263   Date:

_____
_____
_____
_____
_____

Day 264   Date:

_____

_____

_____

_____

_____

Day 265   Date:

_____

_____

_____

_____

_____

Day 266   Date:

_____

_____

_____

_____

_____

Name five things in life that bring you joy?

1. _____

2. _____

3. _____

4. _____

5. _____

Day 206   Date:

_____

_____

_____

_____

_____

Day 207   Date:

_____

_____

_____

_____

_____

Day 208   Date:

_____

_____

_____

_____

_____

Day 209   Date:

_____

_____

_____

_____

Day 210   Date:

_____
_____
_____
_____
_____

Day 211   Date:

_____
_____
_____
_____

Day 212   Date:

_____
_____
_____
_____

Who have you been able to count on for support
in the past? Who is likely to be there for you as you
create what you want for your future?

_____
_____
_____
_____

Choose to find something to be grateful for in each place you visit, every activity you take part in, and with all the people in your life.

Day 213   **Date:**

_____

_____

_____

_____

_____

Day 214   **Date:**

_____

_____

_____

_____

_____

Day 215   **Date:**

_____

_____

_____

_____

_____

Day 216   Date:

_____

_____

_____

_____

_____

Day 217   Date:

_____

_____

_____

_____

_____

Day 218   Date:

_____

_____

_____

_____

_____

Day 219   Date:

_____

_____

_____

_____

Day 220   Date:

_____

_____

_____

_____

_____

Day 221   Date:

_____

_____

_____

_____

_____

Day 222   Date:

_____

_____

_____

_____

_____

Day 223   Date:

_____

_____

_____

_____

Day 224   Date:

_____
_____
_____
_____
_____

Day 225   Date:

_____
_____
_____
_____

If you had a day to do anything you
wanted, what would you choose to do?
What are your favorite things to do?

_____
_____
_____
_____
_____
_____
_____
_____
_____

Day 226   Date:

_____

_____

_____

_____

_____

Day 227   Date:

_____

_____

_____

_____

_____

Day 228   Date:

_____

_____

_____

_____

_____

Day 229   Date:

_____

_____

_____

_____

Day 230   Date:

_____

_____

_____

_____

_____

Day 231   Date:

_____

_____

_____

_____

_____

Day 232   Date:

_____

_____

_____

_____

_____

What sports and hobbies add to the quality of your
life? What would you like to spend more time doing?

_____

_____

_____

_____

_____

Day 233   Date:

_____
_____
_____
_____
_____

Day 234   Date:

_____
_____
_____
_____
_____

Day 235   Date:

_____
_____
_____
_____
_____

Day 236   Date:

_____
_____
_____
_____
_____

Day 237   Date:

_____
_____
_____
_____
_____

Day 238   Date:

_____
_____
_____
_____
_____

Give thanks for your creative spirit; for creative
thoughts, ideas and problem solving, and for the
spark of expression through writing, photography,
artwork, music, cooking, dance, etc.
Where do you enjoy directing your creative energy?
What inspires your creativity?

_____
_____
_____
_____
_____
_____
_____

Day 239   Date:

_____
_____
_____
_____
_____

Day 240   Date:

_____
_____
_____
_____
_____

Day 241   Date:

_____
_____
_____
_____
_____

Day 242   Date:

_____
_____
_____
_____
_____

Day 243   Date:

_____
_____
_____
_____
_____

Day 244   Date:

_____
_____
_____
_____
_____

Day 245   Date:

_____
_____
_____
_____
_____

What are your favorite places to spend time? Where
do you feel most comfortable, happy, and at home?

_____
_____
_____
_____
_____

> *Our lives are not all good, not all bad.*
> *You can find peace when you are able to see*
> *something good in the bad.*

Day 246   **Date:**

_____

_____

_____

_____

_____

Day 247   **Date:**

_____

_____

_____

_____

_____

Day 248   **Date:**

_____

_____

_____

_____

_____

Day 249   Date:

_____
_____
_____
_____

Day 250   Date:

_____
_____
_____
_____

Day 251   Date:

_____
_____
_____
_____

Day 252   Date:

_____
_____
_____
_____

Day 253   Date:

_____

_____

_____

_____

Day 254   Date:

_____

_____

_____

_____

Day 255   Date:

_____

_____

_____

_____

Day 256   Date:

_____

_____

_____

_____

Day 257   Date:

_____
_____
_____
_____
_____

Day 258   Date:

_____
_____
_____
_____
_____

Day 259   Date:

_____
_____
_____
_____
_____

Next time you find yourself in an uncomfortable place, like a doctor's office or stuck in traffic, take a moment to reflect on the things you appreciate or imagine yourself doing something you love.

Day 267					Date:

_____
_____
_____
_____
_____

Day 268					Date:

_____
_____
_____
_____
_____

Day 269					Date:

_____
_____
_____
_____
_____

Day 270					Date:

_____
_____
_____
_____
_____

Day 271   Date:

_____
_____
_____
_____
_____

Day 272   Date:

_____
_____
_____
_____
_____

Day 273   Date:

_____
_____
_____
_____
_____

Find a meaningful gratitude prayer or quote to act
as a warm and gentle reminder of all there is to
appreciate. Look online or in books.

(You can rewrite it or print and paste it onto the
Quotes and Notes pages at the back of this book.)

Day 274   Date:

_____

_____

_____

_____

_____

Day 275   Date:

_____

_____

_____

_____

_____

Day 276   Date:

_____

_____

_____

_____

_____

Day 277   Date:

_____

_____

_____

_____

Day 278   Date:

_____
_____
_____
_____
_____

Day 279   Date:

_____
_____
_____
_____
_____

Day 280   Date:

_____
_____
_____
_____
_____

Write unedited for ten minutes straight
about all the things you appreciate.

(You can use the writing pages
in the back of this book.)

Day 281   Date:

_____

_____

_____

_____

_____

Day 282   Date:

_____

_____

_____

_____

_____

Day 283   Date:

_____

_____

_____

_____

_____

Day 284   Date:

_____

_____

_____

_____

Day 285   Date:

_____
_____
_____
_____
_____

Day 286   Date:

_____
_____
_____
_____
_____

Day 287   Date:

_____
_____
_____
_____
_____

Try something new this week
and appreciate the experience.

_____
_____
_____
_____

Day 288   Date:

_____

_____

_____

_____

_____

Day 289   Date:

_____

_____

_____

_____

_____

Day 290   Date:

_____

_____

_____

_____

_____

Day 291   Date:

_____

_____

_____

_____

Day 292   Date:

_____

_____

_____

_____

_____

Day 293   Date:

_____

_____

_____

_____

Even difficult situations have hidden gifts to be
thankful for. These times can contain blessings
in disguise or opportunities to learn and grow.

Think of a conflict you are experiencing. What benefits
or positives might it offer? What can you be grateful
for in this situation? What might you learn from it?

_____

_____

_____

_____

_____

_____

Day 294   Date:

_____

_____

_____

_____

_____

Day 295   Date:

_____

_____

_____

_____

_____

Day 296   Date:

_____

_____

_____

_____

_____

Day 297   Date:

_____

_____

_____

_____

Day 298   Date:

_____
_____
_____
_____
_____

Day 299   Date:

_____
_____
_____
_____

Expand Your Gratitude: Write a paragraph expanding on your appreciation for something in your life. (For example: I am so truly grateful for the sun. I appreciate the way it lights up the world, makes the tree leaves glow and living things grow. I love the way the sunlight warms me when I'm cool and the way it feels against my skin.)

_____
_____
_____
_____
_____
_____

> *During this week, notice the beauty that surrounds you. Increase your awareness of the images, colors, shapes, and shadows.*

Day 300   **Date:**

_____
_____
_____
_____
_____

Day 301   **Date:**

_____
_____
_____
_____
_____

Day 302   **Date:**

_____
_____
_____
_____
_____

Day 303   Date:

_____

_____

_____

_____

_____

Day 304   Date:

_____

_____

_____

_____

_____

Day 305   Date:

_____

_____

_____

_____

_____

Day 306   Date:

_____

_____

_____

_____

_____

Day 307   Date:

_____

_____

_____

_____

_____

Day 308   Date:

_____

_____

_____

_____

_____

Day 309   Date:

_____

_____

_____

_____

_____

Day 310   Date:

_____

_____

_____

_____

Day 311   Date:

_____

_____

_____

_____

_____

Day 312   Date:

_____

_____

_____

_____

Day 313   Date:

_____

_____

_____

_____

Are there items in your environment that you hardly
notice because they have become part of the background
of your life? Look at your surroundings as if seeing
them for the first time. What do you notice?

_____

_____

_____

Day 314   Date:

_____
_____
_____
_____
_____

Day 315   Date:

_____
_____
_____
_____
_____

Day 316   Date:

_____
_____
_____
_____
_____

Day 317   Date:

_____
_____
_____
_____
_____

Day 318   Date:

_____
_____
_____
_____
_____

Day 319   Date:

_____
_____
_____
_____
_____

Day 320   Date:

_____
_____
_____
_____
_____

What scents do you appreciate most?
The air after it rains? A freshly brewed cup of coffee?
A squirt of lemon?

_____
_____
_____
_____

> *Give thanks for all the things that help you get a good night's sleep such as a cozy and comfortable bed, pillow, blanket, etc.*

Day 321   **Date:**

_____
_____
_____
_____
_____

Day 322   **Date:**

_____
_____
_____
_____
_____

Day 323   **Date:**

_____
_____
_____
_____
_____

Day 324   Date:

_____

_____

_____

_____

Day 325   Date:

_____

_____

_____

_____

Day 326   Date:

_____

_____

_____

_____

Day 327   Date:

_____

_____

_____

_____

Day 328   Date:

_____
_____
_____
_____
_____

Day 329   Date:

_____
_____
_____
_____
_____

Day 330   Date:

_____
_____
_____
_____
_____

Day 331   Date:

_____
_____
_____
_____

Day 332   Date:

_____
_____
_____
_____
_____

Day 333   Date:

_____
_____
_____
_____

What are your favorite sounds?...Rainfall? Birds? Laughter?

_____
_____

Think of what life would be like without music.
What music do you love to hear? Which songs
or pieces of music do you find most uplifting?
Appreciate the artists, songwriters, and composers.

_____
_____
_____
_____
_____

Day 334   Date:

_____

_____

_____

_____

_____

Day 335   Date:

_____

_____

_____

_____

_____

Day 336   Date:

_____

_____

_____

_____

_____

Day 337   Date:

_____

_____

_____

_____

_____

Day 338   Date:

_____
_____
_____
_____
_____

Day 339   Date:

_____
_____
_____
_____
_____

Think of reasons to be thankful for where you live:
the country, city, town or neighborhood.
What benefits are there for living where you do
rather than in other places around the world?

_____
_____
_____
_____
_____
_____
_____

Day 340   Date:

_____
_____
_____
_____
_____

Day 341   Date:

_____
_____
_____
_____
_____

Day 342   Date:

_____
_____
_____
_____
_____

Day 343   Date:

_____
_____
_____
_____
_____

Day 344   Date:

_____
_____
_____
_____
_____

Day 245   Date:

_____
_____
_____
_____

Day 346   Date:

_____
_____
_____
_____
_____

Gratitude Memory Letter: Write a letter of
appreciation to something from the past that's
no longer in your life, such as a beloved childhood
pet, a house you no longer live in, or a cherished
possession that's long gone. Write about the
gifts you received from having had that in your life.

> *People who are grateful experience more happiness. People who are happy feel they have more control over their lives.*

Day 347   **Date:**

_____
_____
_____
_____
_____

Day 348   **Date:**

_____
_____
_____
_____
_____

Day 349   **Date:**

_____
_____
_____
_____
_____

Day 350   Date:

_____

_____

_____

_____

_____

Day 351   Date:

_____

_____

_____

_____

_____

Day 352   Date:

_____

_____

_____

_____

_____

Day 353   Date:

_____

_____

_____

_____

_____

Day 354   Date:

_____

_____

_____

_____

_____

Day 355   Date:

_____

_____

_____

_____

_____

Day 356   Date:

_____

_____

_____

_____

_____

Day 357   Date:

_____

_____

_____

_____

Day 358   Date:

_____
_____
_____
_____
_____

Day 359   Date:

_____
_____
_____
_____

Day 360   Date:

_____
_____
_____
_____

Consider taking a week's vacation from complaining
and negative self-talk. Instead of voicing a complaint,
pause and think of something you are grateful for.
Shift your thinking to the positives in your life.
Work on this over the course of the week and see
how successful you can become. You may even
decide to continue this for another week.

> *One gift opens the door to all the others...Life!*
> *Spend time in gratitude for each breath*
> *you take and for the experience of being alive.*

Day 361   **Date:**

_____

_____

_____

_____

_____

Day 362   **Date:**

_____

_____

_____

_____

_____

Day 363   **Date:**

_____

_____

_____

_____

_____

Day 364   Date:

_____
_____
_____
_____
_____

Day 365   Date:

_____
_____
_____
_____

How has your relationship to gratitude changed since
you began this journal? What activities or experiences
with gratitude have you found to be the most helpful?
What did you get out of this journal?

_____
_____
_____
_____
_____
_____
_____
_____
_____

Continuing the Gratitude Habit

Now that you have completed this journal, begin thinking of what you can do to keep gratitude present in your life.

Here are some ideas:

- Hang a **visual gratitude reminder:** place a photo, magazine image, postcard, or written reminder where you can see it daily; on the refrigerator, door, or mirror.
- Draw, paint, or collage a **visual expression** of gratitude.
- Use the *Quotes and Notes* page (after the *Action Plan*) to keep the meaningful **gratitude quotes** you come upon.
- Establish a **daily gratitude practice** triggered by something you do everyday. For example: Whenever you put on shoes or brush your teeth, wash your face or get the mail, let it remind you to give thanks for that day.
- Carry a **gratitude stone:** a small stone to carry around in your pocket or purse. Choose a stone that you are drawn to. Keep it in its natural state or decorate it with paint or permanent markers.
- Start a **gratitude photo journal** of people, places, things, and experiences you appreciate.
- Keep a **gratitude jar:** Using colorful strips of paper or Post-it notes, put written statements of appreciation into a glass vase or jar. Place the gratitude jar in a visible location as an interactive prompt.
- Use any of the **writing exercises** found in the book.
- **Share your appreciations** with one or more friends. Schedule an appreciation sharing session.
- Use a **whiteboard:** to express gratitude for one or more of the gifts in your life. Hang it in a visible location. Add to it or erase and start over at anytime.
- Find a **prayer of gratitude** you would like to use daily.
- Start **another journal.**

Gratitude Action Plan

Highlight any of the ideas on the prior page you might consider using. What other things can you do to keep gratitude active in your life?

_____

_____

_____

_____

What visual reminder would you find helpful for encouraging a daily gratitude practice?

_____

_____

What gratitude writing activities would you consider using in the future?

_____

_____

What do you plan to do in the coming month to continue your gratitude practice?

_____

_____

_____

What gratitude activities and experiences would you like to be doing during the next 6 months or in the coming year?

_____

_____

_____

_____

Quotes and Notes

These pages can be used for writing quotes, prayers, and words that inspire you.

...more Quotes and Notes

100 Gratitudes

*Here is a blank copy of the **100 Gratitudes** form in case you are interested in generating a second list at some point after you have completed this journal.*

I am grateful for:

1. _____
2. _____
3. _____
4. _____
5. _____
6. _____
7. _____
8. _____
9. _____
10. _____
11. _____
12. _____
13. _____
14. _____
15. _____

16. _____
17. _____
18. _____
19. _____
20. _____
21. _____
22. _____
23. _____
24. _____
25. _____
26. _____
27. _____
28. _____
29. _____
30. _____

I am grateful for:

31. _____
32. _____
33. _____
34. _____
35. _____
36. _____
37. _____
38. _____
39. _____
40. _____
41. _____
42. _____
43. _____
44. _____
45. _____
46. _____
47. _____

48. _____
49. _____
50. _____
51. _____
52. _____
53. _____
54. _____
55. _____
56. _____
57. _____
58. _____
59. _____
60. _____
61. _____
62. _____
63. _____
64. _____
65. _____

I am grateful for:

66.

67.

68.

69.

70.

71.

72.

73.

74.

75.

76.

77.

78.

79.

80.

81.

82.

83.

84.

85.

86.

87.

88.

89.

90.

91.

92.

93.

94.

95.

96.

97.

98.

99.

100.

Writing Pages